Published by Creative Education
P.O. Box 227, Mankato, Minnesota 56002

Creative Education is an imprint of The Creative Company.
Design by Stephanie Blumenthal
Production design by The Design Lab
Art direction by Rita Marshall
Printed in the United States of America

Photographs by Alamy (Tibor Bognar; Core Imagery; Danita Delimont; Bildarchiv
Monheim GmbH; Virginia Fitzherbert; Jon Arnold Images Ltd; Lebrecht Music
and Arts Photo Library; Justine Walker); Corbis (1991 Roger Ressmeyer, Fish
Lamp © Frank Gehry & New City Editions; Robert Holmes; Krista Kennell/
ZUMA; John Edward Linden/Arcaid; Francis G. Mayer; Jacques Pavlovsky/
Sygma; Roger Ressmeyer; Richard Sobol/ZUMA; Ramin Talaie); Getty Images
(American Stock; John W Banagan; Michelle Chaplow; Rick Diamond/WireImage;
Rosmi Duaso//Time Life Pictures; Lambert; DAN LEVINE/AFP; David McNew;
Ralph Orlowski; Scott Olson; Panoramic Images; Bob Riha, Jr./Walt Disney
Concert Hall; Time Life Pictures/Pix Inc./Time Life Pictures; Renaud Visage;
Susan Wood; JUNG YEON-JE/AFP) The Granger Collection, New York

Text on pages 44–45 from "Frank Gehry: Foreshadowing the
Twenty-First Century," by Rappolt, Mark, and Robert Violette, eds.
introduction by Horst Bredekamp, *Gehry Draws*, 950-word excerpt,
© 2004 MIT & Violette Ltd. Used by permission of The MIT Press.

Library of Congress Cataloging-in-Publication Data

Bodden, Valerie.
Frank Gehry / by Valerie Bodden.
p. cm. — (Xtraordinary artists)
Includes index.
ISBN 978-1-58341-662-4
1. Gehry, Frank O., 1929–Juvenile literature. 2. Architects—United States—
Biography—Juvenile literature. I. Title. II. Series.

NA737.G44B58 2008
720'.92—dc22   2007004201

First edition

2 4 6 8 9 7 5 3 1

XTRAORDINARY ARTISTS

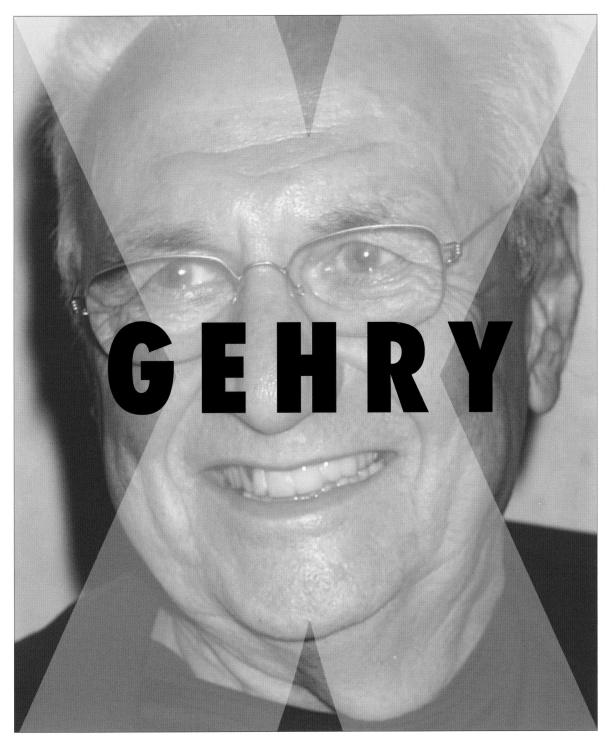

GEHRY

VALERIE BODDEN

CREATIVE 🍎 EDUCATION

His buildings have been called "beautiful" and "offensive," "innovative" and "difficult," "exciting" and "shocking"—all at the same time. But that doesn't bother Frank Gehry; he has never been a conventional architect. Finding his inspiration in art more than in architecture, Gehry has designed some of the world's most bizarre buildings, using cheap materials such as plywood and unconventional shapes such as curves and spirals. The imaginative architect began early in his career to turn his pencil against traditional box-shaped buildings, and he eventually conceived a sinuous, fluid style all his own. Although he never developed this style into a "school" of architecture, it was eventually embraced by critics, architects, and the public alike, who now flock to all corners of the world to see his buildings.

Frank Gehry was born Frank Owen Goldberg (he later changed his surname at the age of 25) on February 28, 1929, in Toronto, Canada. His mother, Thelma, who had studied music at Hamburg Institute in Toronto, began early in Frank's life to instill in him a love for the arts, taking him and his only sibling, younger sister Doreen, to the Art Gallery of Ontario and the Royal Ontario Museum. At the same time, Frank's father, Irving, a former boxer who struggled to find success in one small business after another, saw Frank as a dreamer who wouldn't amount to much. Although he often turned his temper on the young boy, Irving also spent time drawing with his son—time that Frank cherished.

During his youth, Frank spent many hours with his grandparents, who had migrated from Poland to Canada. He considered his grandmother to be his best friend, and the two

Although he was born in Toronto, Frank Gehry would become a global architect, creating works as far away as Dusseldorf, Germany (pictured)

5

6

often sat together on the floor constructing buildings and cities out of odd-shaped scraps of wood. On Thursdays, Frank would go to the market with his grandmother, where she would purchase a carp for the Jewish family's Sabbath supper. When they got home, Frank's grandmother would place the fish in the bathtub, and the boy would sit and watch it the rest of the day, admiring its beautiful, fluid form.

When Frank was in junior high, his father moved the family to the gold-mining town of Timmins in northern Ontario, where he opened a vending and slot machine business. Frank, a shy adolescent who later called himself "the dreamer in the family," spent most of

"Actually, Frank is courteous, considerate, and punctual; that, coupled with his innate generosity and ferocious integrity, makes it impossible to have a bad experience with him."

— *Frank Stella, American painter and sculptor*

Gehry loved the sport of hockey from boyhood; in 2004, he designed the trophy for the World Cup of Hockey, an international tournament

8

his time alone, often with a copy of *Popular Mechanics* in hand, although he also took up the sport of hockey, which would become a lifelong hobby. Frank was an average student but didn't enjoy his new school, where he was the only Jewish boy and was often the victim of anti-Semitism, with classmates bullying him and calling him "Fish-head." The family's stay in Timmins didn't last long, however, as the Canadian government outlawed slot machines in the mid-1940s, putting an end to Irving's business, and the family returned to Toronto.

Back in his hometown, Frank again spent time with his grandparents, working part-time in their hardware store, where he was allowed to tinker with broken items such as toasters and clocks, taking them apart and then reassembling them. Surrounded by the raw tools of the building trade—nuts, bolts, chains, and wood—Frank developed a passion for these workaday materials that would stay with him, even as his family faced yet another move.

This time, the family, looking for a healthier climate after Irving suffered a heart

attack—and broke as a result of his multiple business failures upon their return to Toronto—headed for Los Angeles, California, which was experiencing an economic boom in the wake of World War II. The Goldbergs rented a small two-room apartment in a run-down area of the city, and Frank's mother found a job in a department store. Frank, who was now 18, took a job driving trucks and installing breakfast nooks in people's homes.

Although the difficult situation with his father during his last year in Toronto—including the task of helping his mother auction off his father's assets—had kept Frank from finishing his fifth year of high school and graduating, he began taking night classes at the University of Southern California (USC). Because a fifth year of high school in Canada

Besides its architecture program, the University of Southern California is also famous for its cinematic school, producing many filmmakers

11

was equivalent to the first year of college in the United States, Frank found it easy to slip into college life in his new home. Unsure of what kind of career to pursue, Frank focused his classes in the university's fine arts program, which included a ceramics course taught by Glenn Lukens, a well-known local artist who quickly became a mentor to Frank.

At the time, Lukens was having a house built by Raphael Soriano, a renowned Modernist architect, and he invited Frank to the building site to watch Soriano work. What Frank saw left him, in his words, "lit up": Soriano, a short man wearing a beret, was yelling at contractors to get them to move walls. After this experience, Frank switched majors, enrolling in the university's School of Architecture. He had found his calling.

Once enrolled in the architecture program at USC, Frank threw himself wholeheartedly into his training, spending Sundays driving around L.A. to study the houses discussed in his classes. In 1952, while he was still in school, 23-year-old Frank married Anita Snyder, whom he had met while working at the breakfast nook company. Anita took a job as a legal secretary to help pay Frank's school bills, and two years later, the two were expecting their first daughter, Leslie, when Frank graduated with honors. That same year, Anita convinced Frank to change his last name to Gehry—a name she invented—in order to shield their children from anti-Semitism. Although Frank agreed to the change, he later confessed that he always regretted it.

After his graduation from USC, Frank served briefly as an architect in charge of recreational services in the Army. Then, in 1956, he and his young family—which now also included a second daughter, Brina—moved to Cambridge, Massachusetts, where he enrolled in a post-graduate program in city planning at Harvard University.

By studying city planning, Frank hoped to learn how to bring about social change through innovative, affordable housing designs. After less than a year, however, Frank dropped out of the program, disillusioned with its theoretical nature, and began to attend lectures that appealed to his imagination. Through these lectures, Frank was introduced to the work of Swiss-born architect Le Corbusier, whose Notre-Dame-du-Haut chapel in

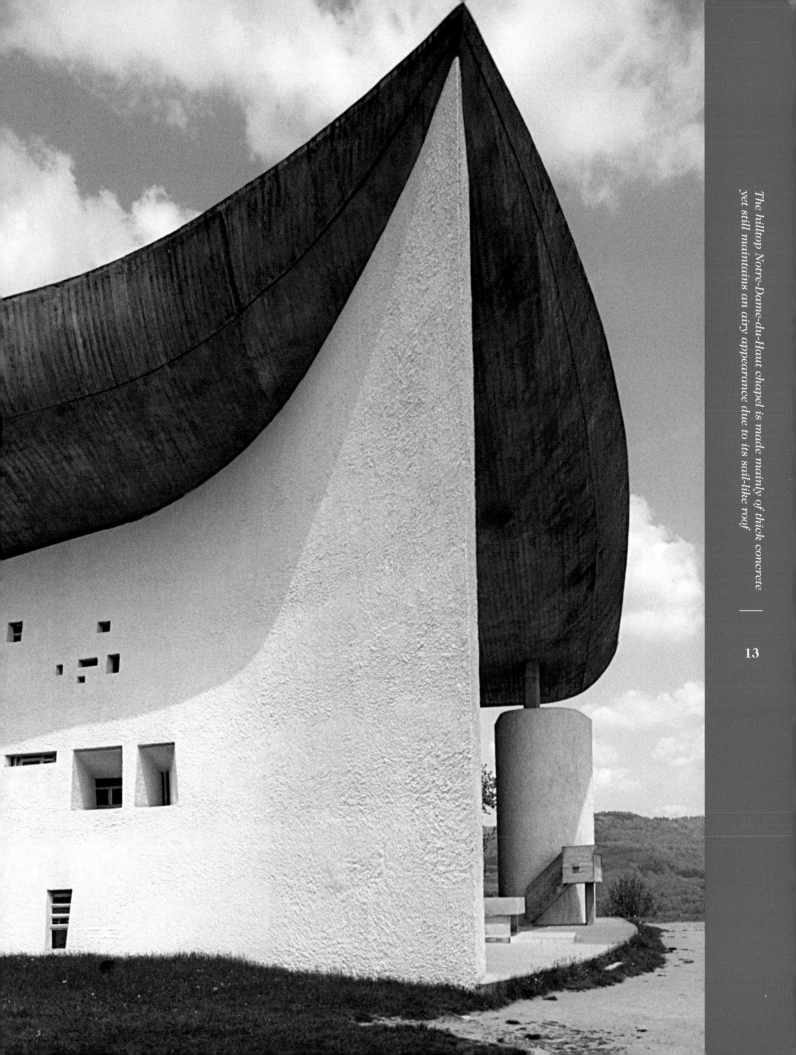

The hilltop Notre-Dame-du-Haut chapel is made mainly of thick concrete yet still maintains an airy appearance due to its sail-like roof

13

Ronchamp, France—with its coarse masonry walls and dramatic curved roof—thrilled him. "That's when I threw the grid away," Frank later recalled, "and said, 'Man, there's another freedom out there, and that's the place I want to be.'"

In the spring of 1957, Frank moved his family back to L.A., where he worked for two large architectural firms before deciding in 1961 to move to Paris. There, Frank worked for the firm of André Remondet for a year before returning to L.A., where, at the age of 33, he opened his own firm, Frank O. Gehry and Associates, focusing mainly on commercial buildings.

Even as his architectural business began to take off, however, Frank found himself spending time not with other architects, but with artists such as Ed Kienholz and Ed Ruscha. He found that he had more in common with these painters and sculptors, who were experimenting with making art out of everyday objects, than with other architects. Eager to

"There are no gloomy Gehry buildings.... These are light and lively designs and buildings that lift the spirit with revelations of how the seemingly ordinary can become extraordinary by acts of imagination.... He will continue ... turning the practical into the lyrical, and architecture into art."

— *American architecture critic Ada Louise Huxtable*

experiment as he saw his artist friends doing, Frank continued his commercial work while also taking on more unusual "sideline" projects to nurture his creativity. One of his first such projects, completed in 1965, was the Danziger Studio and Residence in Hollywood, for which Frank designed two separate cube-shaped buildings (one a house and one a studio) linked by a garden wall.

Even as his professional life was moving forward, though, Frank's personal life was unraveling, and he began to see Milton Wexler, a noted psychoanalyst. Wexler immediately observed that Frank's marriage was "in limbo" and encouraged the architect to either commit to his wife or leave the marriage immediately. Frank decided to leave, and he and Anita divorced in 1968.

That same year, a young Panamanian woman named Berta Isabel Aguilera arrived at Frank's office for a job interview. Although she ultimately turned the job down, she had caught Frank's attention, and the 39-year-old asked her out to dinner. Seven years later, in 1975, the two were married.

In 1976, Berta gave birth to the couple's first son, Alejandro. With Alejandro's birth, the expanding family (Samuel would be born in 1979) soon outgrew its apartment and moved into a two-story, 1920s-era house, on which Berta encouraged her husband to experiment. So, with $40,000 and lots of ideas, Frank set about remodeling their home, building an L-shaped addition of corrugated metal and plywood around the existing exterior. He also stripped down some of the interior walls, leaving exposed frames, beams, and joists, reflecting his belief that "buildings look most interesting before they are finished."

Although residents in Frank's middle-class neighborhood abhorred his addition, influential architects and artists rushed to tour the house. In 1980, the American Institute of Architects chose the residence for its Honor Award, recognizing it as an "expansion of the American Dream into new areas."

Around the time Frank finished work on his house, he also completed a $50-million shopping mall in Santa Monica for a developer client. When the client visited Frank's remodeled home, he remarked that if Frank liked his house, he couldn't possibly like the more conventional commercial work he was doing and made the radical suggestion that Frank stop building malls. Far from being offended, Frank took the advice to heart. From that point on, he refused projects that required him to compromise his architectural style.

Although the decision was liberating, it was also frightening. At the age of 50, Frank was basically starting over, and with a much smaller client market. Within a month, he had cut his office staff from 40 to 3. Fortunately, Frank had established a reputation by then, and clients looking for something unusual gradually began to turn to him.

One of the first such clients was Loyola Marymount University in L.A. Because the university wanted its law school's campus to make a statement about the study of law, Frank incorporated abstractions of the broken columns of the Roman Forum into his design. Using materials as varied as stucco, brick, and copper sheet metal, Frank created the feeling of a small, close-knit town, or what he called "a village of forms."

Soon, Frank was bringing in larger and larger commissions. At the same time, however, he continued to work on individual residences. Although Frank had once dreamed of

Many of Gehry's early commercial projects, such as the Santa Monica mall pictured here, showed only hints of the grander creativity yet to come

19

creating affordable housing for the poor, he gave up that idea after discovering that social

housing programs in America had more to do with politics than with architectural inno-

vation. As he began to take on projects from wealthy clients instead, Frank found that he

enjoyed the freedom of experimenting with new forms on their houses. One of the most

successful of these houses was the Norton Residence in Venice, California. Completed in

1984, the house consisted of several stacked volumes of concrete block, stucco, and tile. Its most prominent feature, however, was a freestanding study that mimicked the life-guard stations near the beachfront lot.

As Frank's reputation continued to grow, he was asked to design even more extraordinary buildings, including a headquarters complex for the Chiat/Day advertising

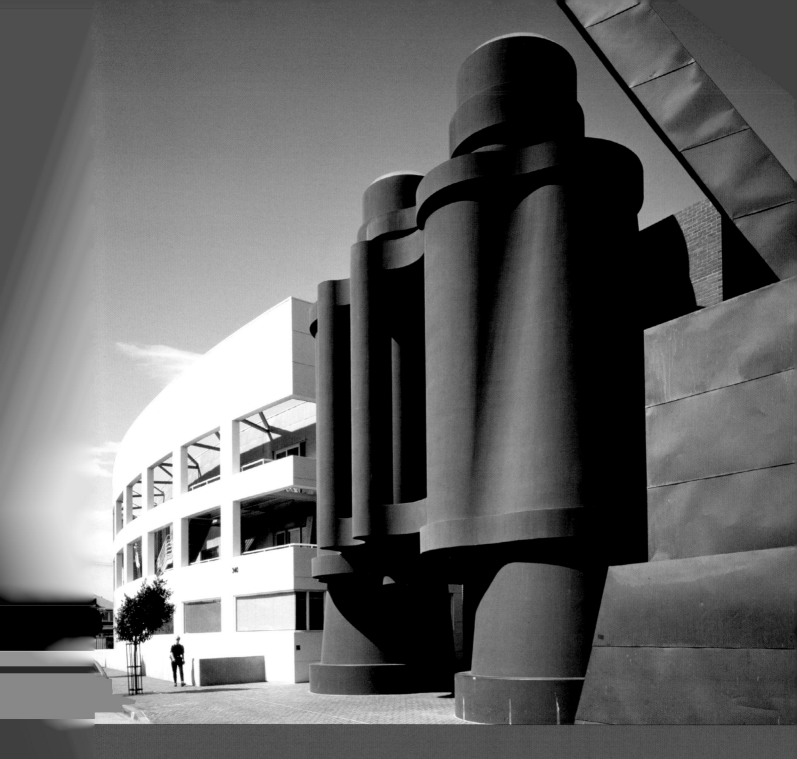

company, also in Venice, for which he came up with a structure composed of three pieces: one boat-shaped, one in the form of abstracted trees, and between them, a building in the shape of a giant pair of binoculars. For this project, Frank took a step almost unheard of in architecture and collaborated with sculptors Claes Oldenburg and Coosje van Bruggen, who helped to design the binocular-shaped building.

Soon after beginning work on the Chiat/Day building in 1985, Frank took on a number of foreign commissions, including the Vitra Design Museum in Germany. In this

"I've always wanted to be involved with architecture and with architects, but I've always found architects rather forbidding and unsympathetic to artists. This is not true of Frank. Frank is very, very welcoming and open to artistic ideas."

— *Swedish-American sculptor Claes Oldenburg*

structure, Frank's style underwent a noticeable shift, as he began to incorporate fluid curves that seemed to capture the movement of the fish he had once observed in his grandmother's bathtub.

After the Vitra Design Museum, Frank's designs became even more curvaceous, which, in turn, made them harder to build. As a result, in the late 1980s, Frank's firm began to look into computer software, eventually purchasing the program CATIA (Computer-Assisted Three-Dimensional Interactive Application) in 1991. With this program, Frank could continue his normal design process—first drawing chaotic-looking sketches, then building model after model from cardboard and paper. Now, though, his staff members could pass a laser pen over the models. The pen then transmitted the coordinates to the

computer program, which created detailed drawings of the building and calculated its components to within an accuracy of 0.04 inches (1 mm).

Even as he was exploring the possibilities of computer-aided design, Frank's willingness to push the envelope in architecture was honored with the 1989 Pritzker Prize, architecture's highest award. Although this award is usually presented to an architect near the end of his or her career, the prize jury said that it hoped the 60-year-old architect would look upon the honor as "encouragement for continuing an extraordinary *work in progress*." After using the $100,000 prize money to make a down payment on a house for his mother, Frank turned back to this "work in progress," soon designing his most extraordinary building yet.

On October 19, 1997, locals and foreigners alike lined the streets of the port city of Bilbao, Spain, waiting in line for hours not to see a famous band or a celebrated dignitary, but to get a first look at something much more monumental—the new Guggenheim Bilbao, a contemporary art museum associated with the famous Guggenheim in New York City designed by Frank Lloyd Wright. This Guggenheim, though, had been designed by another Frank—Frank Gehry—in a process that had begun in 1991.

The Guggenheim Bilbao came out of a plan hatched by the government of Bilbao to embark on a $1.5-billion renovation of the city, which had once been the richest in Spain

but was marked by widespread unemployment by the early 1990s. As part of their urban renewal plan, officials wanted to create a new railway, a redesigned airport, a new performing arts center, and, as the *pièce de résistance*, a new Guggenheim art museum. Together with Thomas Krens, the head of the Guggenheim in New York, the officials held a limited design competition, after which they invited Frank to design the building, which was to be set along the Nervión River.

By February 1993, Frank's design for the museum was complete, and in October of that year, the foundation stone was laid. Soon, an unorthodox structure—more sculpture than building—began to take shape along the riverfront, its rectangular base of Spanish

limestone giving way to curving forms clad in titanium. Depending on the light conditions, the titanium appeared to change color throughout the day, from gold to red to deep blue or gray. At the eastern end of the structure, cars seemed to travel in and out of the museum, as one of its galleries was constructed underneath the Puente de la Salve Bridge, ending in a striking V-shaped tower and visually connecting the Guggenheim to the lifeblood of the city.

The Guggenheim Bilbao was no less astonishing inside. Visitors stepping in through the front doors on the museum's opening day were met with a stunning 160-foot-high (49 m)

atrium decorated in limestone and titanium, with huge windows to let in natural light. Curving bridges, glass-enclosed elevators, and stair towers passed through the atrium, connecting it to the museum's 19 galleries. Somewhat surprisingly, 10 of the galleries were rectangular, much like those in a traditional museum. Others, though, were circular or oval-shaped, and one, designed to accommodate even the largest works of art, measured approximately 425 feet (130 m) long, 100 feet (30 m) wide, and 85 feet (26 m) high.

Although some feared that the museum's riveting architecture would take away from the art inside, Frank's intention was the opposite. He wanted to create a building that would be one with the artwork, which included pieces by Spanish sculptor Eduardo Chillida, Dutch-born American painter Willem de Kooning, and American sculptor Richard Serra. By many accounts, he succeeded, as various artists wrote to thank Frank for creating a "cathedral for art."

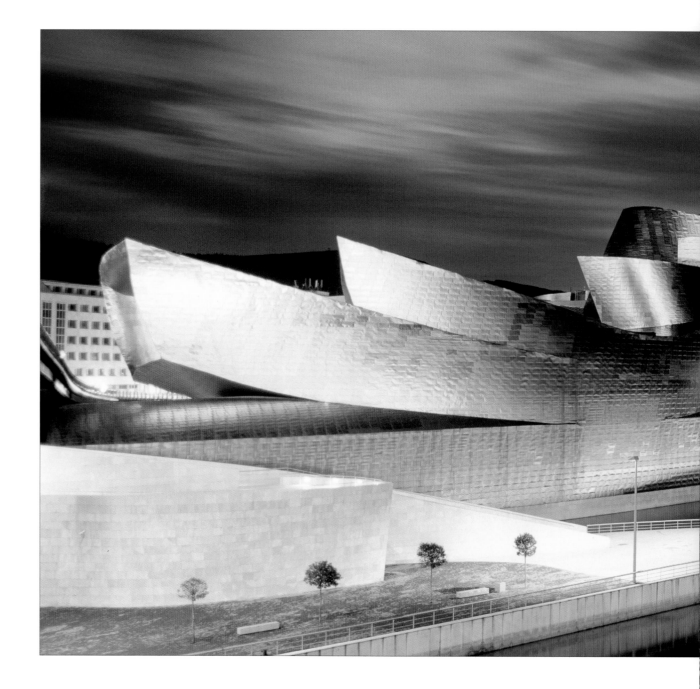

The 265,000-square-foot (24,600 sq m) Guggenheim Bilbao won universal acclaim for the way it seemed both classical and totally unique at once

Artists weren't the only ones impressed by the building. People from around the world streamed into Bilbao to see the Guggenheim. Within a year of its opening, more than a million people had already come to admire the structure, bringing new vitality to the city's economy and creating what came to be known as the "Bilbao effect." Architecture critics hailed the museum as a "miracle," magazines around the world featured the building on their covers, and Philip Johnson, the "dean of American architecture," called it "the greatest building of our time."

"With Bilbao, Gehry came of age as an architect. Scale, design, sophistication, elegance, and the power to communicate with everyman all came together to bring his work to a new level of magisterial prominence and creative command."

— *Guggenheim Museum director Thomas Krens*

Although no one could quite seem to put their finger on what the building resembled—metaphors ranged from "a pile of improbably huge fish" to "a cubist sculpture of a ship" to "an artichoke"—most seemed to agree that it was praiseworthy. And that's what Frank couldn't quite understand: "I'm so used to getting flak for my work that the acceptance of Bilbao has been amazing. If it had happened when I was 40, I'd have been freaked, but I'll be 70 next February [1999], and I'm old enough to take it." Fortunately for Frank, he had learned to "take" the public's acceptance. He was about to get a lot of it.

"We wanted this building to be of the same quality as its contents, with an importance equal to that of the artworks it would eventually house. Over these years, I have been pleased, and to a certain extent astonished, to see the actual project exceeding our ambitions."

— *Juan Ignacio Vidarte, director of Guggenheim Bilbao*

With the revelation of his stunning design for the Guggenheim Bilbao, Frank found himself in high demand, and people who had never before heard of this white-haired architect in the slightly rumpled suit were suddenly clamoring for him to build their next big museum or office building. In 1995, Frank began work on the DG Bank Building in Berlin, Germany, which, on the outside, looked like a marked change from the Guggenheim. Because of strict zoning laws, Frank covered the front of the building in a conservative limestone façade. Inside, however, the mixed-use commercial and residential building was one of the most unusual Frank had yet designed, containing a conference hall set inside a four-story hollow sculpture shaped like a horse's head.

The same year he began work on the DG Bank Building, Frank also took on the Experience Music Project, the brainchild of Microsoft cofounder Paul Allen. A rock-and-roll museum located next to the Space Needle in Seattle, Washington, the Experience Music Project design was composed of six "swoopy" shapes, each a different color, intended to vaguely resemble a smashed guitar. A monorail running through the building offered riders a preview of the museum and linked the structure to the city.

Even as he concentrated on these large projects, Frank was also working on a smaller project close to his heart: a practice rink in Anaheim, California, for the city's National Hockey League team, the Mighty Ducks. The architect—who continued to enjoy playing

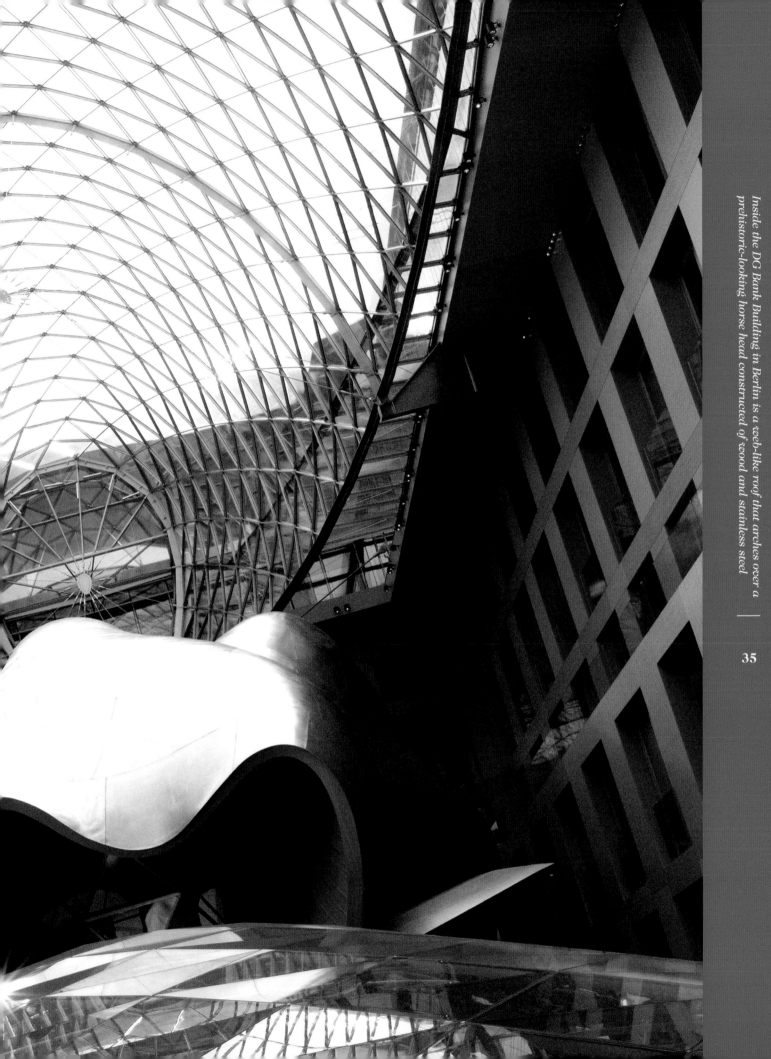

Inside the DG Bank Building in Berlin is a web-like roof that arches over a prehistoric-looking horse head constructed of wood and stainless steel

35

hockey with his sons at the age of 66 and even sponsored his own semiprofessional team, the FOG—confessed that he concentrated more on the interior of the rink than the exterior because he knew he was going to be skating there. With wooden beams covering the ceiling, the rink (originally known as Disney Ice and now called Anaheim Ice) offered a warm feeling reminiscent of the rinks Frank grew up with in Canada.

As he worked on designing these new projects, Frank was also trying to complete a project that he had begun even before the Guggenheim. In 1989, Frank had started work

on the Walt Disney Concert Hall in downtown L.A., but, due to fundraising problems, the building's completion was delayed for more than a decade. Finally, in 2003, work was completed on the concert hall, a huge building of curvaceous steel-clad forms. Although the building received high praise for its sound system—which Frank had painstakingly worked out with acousticians—its architecture received mixed reviews; one critic called it "half-torn-up cardboard boxes spray-painted silver."

Like the Walt Disney Concert Hall, a good number of Frank's buildings have

Although Gehry's unusual style has never pleased all critics, it has made him what some have called a "starchitect" in countries around the world

met with criticism from detractors, who have called his works "ugly," "perverse," and "oppressive." Yet by 2008, Frank still had a huge fan base and remained in high demand, with plans in the works for Atlantic Yards, a development in Brooklyn, New York, that included a new basketball arena, housing units, and retail stores; the Grand Avenue Project, a revitalization effort to bring nightlife to downtown L.A.; and a possible new Guggenheim museum in the Middle Eastern country of the United Arab Emirates. One of the most meaningful projects on Frank's drawing board was the design for a new performing arts center at Ground Zero in New York City.

"There are many reasons we're interested in Gehry. For one: When you see what Frank is doing, the kind of architecture, the emotion he puts into it, when you look at it, you realize it hasn't been done before. Whether you like it or not is irrelevant. There is artistic power in the shapes."

— *Bernard Charles, president of Dassault Systèmes, maker of CATIA*

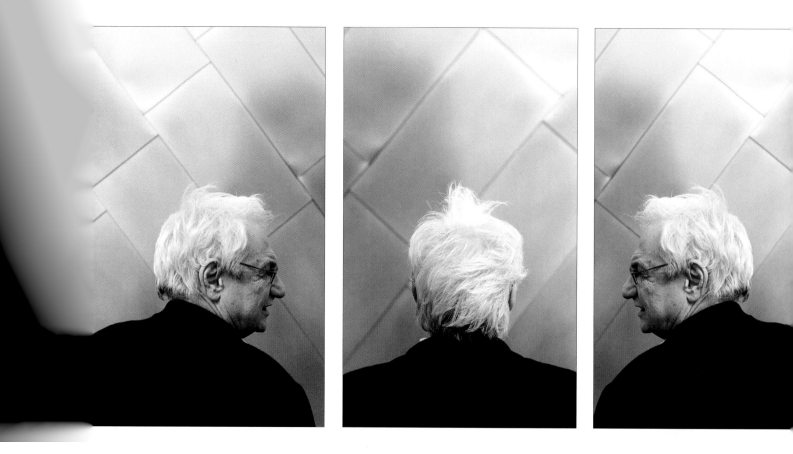

Even with more than 175 staff members in his firm (including his son Samuel for a time), Frank continued to design every one of these projects himself, showing no signs of slowing down with his work as he approached his 80th birthday. In fact, he said in 1999 that his creativity was picking up speed, as he tried more and more to capture movement in his buildings, while also increasingly collaborating with artists (including his son Alejandro) and other architects.

Not satisfied to rest on the laurels of the more than 100 awards he has received during his career, Frank continues to push himself to come up with new, better designs. "You can't redo old ideas," he said. "The only way to gain is to go forward and not look back. You can learn from the past, but you can't continue to be in the past." One thing is certain: Frank Gehry has never been accused of being an architect of the past, and his works are likely to be renowned far into the future.

"In an artistic climate that too often looks backward rather than toward the future, ... it is important to honor the architecture of Frank O. Gehry. Refreshingly original and totally American, ... Gehry's work is a highly refined, sophisticated, and adventurous aesthetic that emphasizes the art of architecture."

— *Pritzker Prize jury citation*

Unlike many other famous architects, Frank Gehry has never promoted a specific style or "school" of architecture. He has not churned out books or papers espousing his architectural theories or justifying his form, preferring instead to focus his time and energy on his designs. Yet, this has not stopped architecture critics from analyzing and attempting to explain Gehry's style.

The following excerpt from an essay by virtual reality filmmaker Rene Daalder for the 2004 book *Gehry Draws* focuses on Gehry as a pioneer of the Digital Age and on the differing perceptions of his work among architects and the general public.

When I first looked at Gehry's drawings my mind instantly connected his artistic scribbles to the computer as the perfect medium to analyze and translate his inimitable gestures into architecture. When a trained handwriting expert can analyze the highly personal flourishes of the human hand,... then it seems entirely reasonable to suggest that a computer can translate and interpret them just as well. In fact, this is a task that millions of computers perform every day, checking the authenticity of credit card signatures and performing all kinds of handwriting recognition tasks for intelligence agencies across the globe.

[My focus in this essay] will be to establish Frank Gehry's importance as a trailblazer for the digital age. When we met, however, I was surprised at how reluctant he was to consider himself a digital pioneer. Although he did credit the computer for playing a major role in his organizational process, providing him with the upper hand in the often-contentious relationship between architects and "parental" developers, he looked at the computer primarily as a number-crunching machine rather than an active participant in his creative process.

I told him that on an intuitive level he may be much more connected to the computer's digital intelligence than he thinks and that the popular perception of his work as computer-driven architecture may indeed be more to the point than his own attitude toward the technology suggests. Even though Gehry was willing to listen, he wasn't quite prepared to accept the visionary mantle he so clearly deserves, leaving it up to me to articulate his importance for the digital era regardless of his own day-to-day relationship with the computer.... It is interesting to note that every architectural expert who writes about [Gehry's] creative process focuses on the fact that the computer is merely a stepping stone. The cover copy of the book Gehry Talks even goes out of its way to proclaim that "the computer is a tool, not a partner, an instrument for catching the curve, not for inventing it." As I will demonstrate, however, the general public has a distinctly different impression.

The appreciation of Gehry's work by his peers often doesn't seem to measure up to his tremendous popular success. In the course of writing this chapter I came across considerable criticism heaped upon Gehry from within the architectural community. One writer I know described the Walt Disney Concert Hall in Los Angeles... as a stack of tissues thrown away by someone with a head cold, while a prominent young Dutch architect's reluctant visit to the building only produced the disdainful comment that the stainless-steel surfaces were sloppily applied. A quick poll among architecture students at Sci-Arc [Southern California Institute of Architecture] in L.A. had equally lukewarm results.... Around the same time, former New York Times architecture critic and sometime Gehry fan Herbert Muschamp saw fit to describe Gehry's Experience Music Project building in Seattle... as "something that crawled out of the sea, rolled over, and died."

By contrast, an arbitrary sampling of the public's response to the Disney Concert Hall showed that people outside of the profession have a much deeper connection to the building than to most other architecture they ever encountered. During the building's official unveiling its reception was positively ecstatic. One sophisticated connoisseur of art I know admitted that she cried upon coming face to face with the strikingly different architecture, while a talented young screenwriter of my acquaintance went so far as to break down the most important milestones in the history of architecture as follows: "First there was pyramid builder Imhotep, next came the Renaissance architect Palladio, and now, at the dawn of the Digital Age, we have Frank Gehry."

Whatever we might think of these opinions, one thing stands out within the public's reaction to Gehry's work: they appear to be most affected by those buildings that represent the biggest departure from the Modernist aesthetic, such as the Guggenheim Museum in Bilbao... and Disney Concert Hall, both of which are perceived as somehow strongly associated with the computer.... It is as if the people beholding the complex shape of Gehry's buildings are infused with a deep sense of longing for the future....

It may be appropriate to look at Frank Gehry as a defining architect of our historical moment, a man who is intuitively in touch with the future as it is implied by the present....

Frank Gehry has managed intuitively to stay ahead of the game. From his spontaneous sketches to the folds and creases of waxed cloth, the architect has been introducing elements from the actual into the virtual realm all along. Ironically, the critic who compared the Disney Concert Hall to a stack of discarded tissues was unwittingly voicing his appreciation of Gehry's sampling techniques....

As mentioned before, Gehry acknowledges his debt to the computer to the extent that it allows him always to be a few steps ahead of the developers by knowing far in advance what it will take to deliver his buildings on time and on budget. This has had a tremendously liberating effect on him and has been the key to his current productivity, unparalleled by anyone of his stature today.

1929

Frank Owen Goldberg (later changed to Gehry) is born in Toronto, Canada, on February 28.

1947

Gehry moves to Los Angeles, where he studies first fine art, then architecture, at the University of Southern California.

1952

Gehry marries Anita Snyder; their first of two children is born two years later.

1954

Gehry graduates from USC at the top of his class, holding a Bachelor of Architecture degree.

1956

After beginning to study city planning at Harvard, Gehry becomes disillusioned with the theoretical program and drops out.

1961

Gehry moves to Paris to work for architect André Remondet.

1962

After moving back to L.A., Gehry opens his own firm, Frank O. Gehry and Associates.

1965

One of Gehry's first significant commissions, the Danziger Studio and Residence, is completed.

1968

Gehry and Anita divorce; he begins to date Panamanian Berta Isabel Aguilera.

1975

Gehry marries Berta; their first of two sons is born the next year.

1978

A provocative remodel of his house in the Los Angeles suburb of Santa Monica brings Gehry fame.

1984

Gehry completes work on the Norton Residence in Venice, California.

1989

Gehry wins the Pritzker Prize, worth $100,000.

1991

The purchase of CATIA, a computer software program that maps models, enables Gehry to design more curvaceous structures.

1997

The Guggenheim Bilbao opens and is hailed as an architectural "miracle."

2000

The Experience Music Project in Seattle, Washington, opens.

2006

Gehry unveils the design for the Grand Avenue Project, a revitalization effort in downtown Los Angeles.

André Remondet — *A French architect who attended the École Nationale Supèrieure des Beaux-Arts, one of the world's most elite art schools, where he won a prestigious scholarship to study at the French Academy in Rome*

anti-Semitism — *Prejudice against or persecution of Jews, based on their ethnicity and religion*

Claes Oldenburg — *A Swedish-born American sculptor known for his larger-than-life sculptures of everyday objects; he was married to artist Coosje van Bruggen*

Coosje van Bruggen — *A Dutch-born American author and artist known for her collaborations with husband Claes Oldenburg*

Ed Kienholz — *An American sculptor who used everyday objects to create life-sized sculptures*

Ed Ruscha — *An American artist known for paintings and drawings featuring words and phrases; some of his drawings were made from materials such as gunpowder or vegetable juice*

façade — *The main face of a building, which shows its major architectural features*

Ground Zero — *The site of the former World Trade Center towers in New York City, which were destroyed when terrorists flew hijacked airplanes into the buildings on September 11, 2001*

Le Corbusier — *The professional name of Swiss-French architect Charles Édouard Jeanneret, who helped to create the International Style of the 1920s and '30s, which involved the use of simple forms made of glass, steel, and concrete*

Modernist — *Having to do with the architecture of the late 19th and early 20th centuries, characterized in general by a rejection of earlier architecture and an emphasis on the function of a building over its form*

Roman Forum — *A complex at the center of ancient Rome, consisting of temples, businesses, and the Roman court system*

Sabbath — *The weekly day of rest in the Jewish religion, observed from before sundown on Friday until after sunset on Saturday, during which Jews are not supposed to do certain types of work*

Bechtler, Cristina, ed. *Frank O. Gehry – Kurt W. Forster: Art and Architecture, a Dialogue.* Ostfildern-Ruit, Germany: Cantz, 1999.

Chollet, Laurence B. *The Essential Frank O. Gehry.* New York: Wonderland Press, 2001.

Friedman, Mildred, ed. *Gehry Talks: Architecture + Process.* New York: Rizzoli International Publications, 1999.

Greenberg, Jan, and Sandra Jordan. *Frank O. Gehry: Outside In.* New York: DK Publishing, 2000.

Lazo, Caroline Evensen. *Frank Gehry.* Minneapolis: Twenty-First Century Books, 2006.

Miller, Jason. *Frank Gehry.* New York: MetroBooks, 2002.

Ragheb, J. Fiona, ed. *Frank Gehry, Architect.* New York: Guggenheim Museum Publications, 2001.